D0856185

Eyewitness to World
War I medicine /

33387005702735

J 940.3 E

EYEWITNESS TO
WORLD WAR I
MEDICINE

BY EMILY O'KEEFE

Published by The Child's World®
1980 Lookout Drive • Mankato, MN 56003-1705
800-599-READ • www.childsworld.com

Photographs ©: Everett Historical/Shutterstock Images, cover, 1, 5, 14, 24, 26;
AP Images, 6; Ken Welsh/Newscom, 8; National Museum of Health and Medicine,
10; Alinari Archives/Getty Images, 13; Oxford Science Archive Heritage Images/
Newscom, 16, 28; Stefan Sauer/Picture-Alliance/DPA/AP Images, 19; Popperfoto/
Getty Images, 20; Sueddeutsche Zeitung Photo/Alamy, 22; Sammlung Sauer/
Picture-Alliance/ZB/Newscom, 23

ISBN 9781503816107

LCCN 2016945601

Printed in the United States of America
PA02317

ABOUT THE AUTHOR

Emily O'Keefe is a writer and editor who enjoys learning about history,
literature, and culture. She holds a PhD in English from Loyola University.
O'Keefe lives in Chicago, Illinois.

TABLE OF CONTENTS

FAST FACTS

What role did doctors, nurses, and hospitals play in World War I (1914-1918)?

- Medical workers traveled to battlefields. They provided immediate help for injured soldiers.
- Hospital staff provided care for soldiers with serious wounds.

What kinds of injuries did soldiers have?

- During the war, certain dangerous weapons were used for the first time. Medical workers often treated soldiers injured by tank and machine-gun fire. Many soldiers also suffered from the effects of gas attacks.

What other health problems affected soldiers?

- In **trench warfare**, soldiers faced damp, dirty conditions. Rats and lice in the trenches carried diseases. Many soldiers became sick in the trenches.
- An influenza **epidemic** infected 500 million people. Many soldiers and civilians became very sick or even died.
- Infections were also a problem. Wounds that were not treated quickly could become infected.

How did medicine change during World War I?

- X-rays were used widely for the first time. They helped doctors locate and treat wounds.

- The motorized ambulance was invented 15 years before the war began. The ambulance allowed people to get to the hospital more quickly, saving lives.

- Improved **sanitation** methods helped prevent the spread of disease.

- **Triage** helped doctors decide which patients needed the most help.

Chapter 1

DRIVING INTO DANGER

John Masefield could hear the rattle of machine-gun fire. He was driving his ambulance to the battlefield. Explosives burst around the vehicle as he neared the **front**. "One hears . . . the scream of the rush of the big **shells**, the thump of the bursts, and the crash of the great guns," Masefield later wrote.[1] Masefield's ambulance was entering a dangerous area, but he had a job to do.

◄ **Ambulances were the fastest way to transport wounded soldiers from the front to field hospitals.**

Together with other ambulance drivers, Masefield arrived at the battlefield. Injured soldiers stumbled to a makeshift operating room, looking pale. Medical workers loaded wounded men onto stretchers. After the stretchers were in the ambulances, it was time to drive back through the gunfire. "The drivers start their engines and turn the cars for home," Masefield recalled. "Along the road in front of them the shells flash at intervals, lighting the tree stumps."[2]

By the time of this ambulance ride, it was 1916. World War I had been raging for two years. It was unlike any other war in history. Dozens of nations were involved in the conflict. Millions of soldiers had been wounded or killed. New military technologies were transforming warfare. Soldiers carried machine guns, which quickly sprayed hundreds of bullets. Powerful tanks toppled barbed wire on their way to attack enemy forces. Deadly poison gas attacks caused devastating injuries.

Masefield was a poet. He was too old to fight in the war. But his desire to help soldiers led him to join the American Ambulance Field Service. This organization included thousands of volunteer drivers.

Ambulance drivers faced serious dangers. Masefield made many trips through gunfire. Uneven terrain with holes from grenade explosions caused his ambulance to bump and shake.

Despite the dangers, Masefield's efforts benefitted many soldiers. His ambulance quickly brought soldiers to first-aid stations. There, doctors could use better equipment than that which could be used in the field.

"A French captain remarked that, no matter how much the town was being shelled, the little field ambulances could be seen slipping down the streets, past corners, or across the square."

—James R. McConnell, American ambulance driver in Verdun, France[3]

Masefield and other medical workers saved the lives of soldiers and civilians. But after a tough night, Masefield had little time to think about his work. He would be back the next night, driving through the darkness and the bursting shells to help injured soldiers.

◄ John Masefield was old enough to be excused from military service, but he chose to volunteer as an ambulance driver and hospital orderly during the war.

Chapter 2

CARING FOR THE WOUNDED

It was British surgeon John Hayward's first day as a war surgeon. Working at a medical tent in Amiens, France, Hayward quickly became overwhelmed. By 7:00 a.m., the tent was filled with injured soldiers. "I have had no instructions on how to dispose of such numbers," Hayward said.[4] Hayward knew he had to find out which soldiers needed help right away. This would help his staff save the most lives.

◄ Triage helped medical workers prioritize patients based on their injuries.

Hayward and other medical workers during World War I began using a system known as triage. Following this system, Hayward classified soldiers into three groups.

The first group included soldiers with only mild injuries. They could be treated quickly. These soldiers would then go back to fighting. Soldiers in the second group had more serious injuries. They needed more medical attention. Ambulance drivers transported them to hospitals. Soldiers in the third group had very severe injuries. These soldiers were unlikely to survive their wounds. However, nurses and other medical workers did their best to make the soldiers feel comfortable and at ease.

Dividing soldiers into groups allowed Hayward and other doctors to focus their attention on soldiers who needed them most. But even with the triage system, doctors often went days without rest. Hayward's first shift as a war surgeon lasted 36 hours.

Doctors such as Hayward often worked at field hospitals. These were temporary structures close to battlefields. Many soldiers were treated at field hospitals. But soldiers with severe injuries were often sent to regular hospitals for long-term care.

Some field hospitals were nearly as well equipped as other hospitals. But others were missing important equipment.

Stefan Westmann was a German medical officer. By 1918 some German field hospitals were running out of crucial supplies. In Merville, France, Westmann was amazed to discover an abandoned British field hospital. It contained many of the supplies he needed.

"I saw for the first time [in] years the abundance of material, of equipment," Westmann recalled. "Amongst other things I found cases full of surgical gloves."[5] Surgical gloves are important for safety. Doctors need them to prevent infection and the spread of disease. Westmann saved as many cases of gloves and bandages as he could from the abandoned hospital. He used these supplies to help tend to wounded soldiers.

Getting supplies was not the only challenge for field hospitals. Many field hospitals were on rough terrain. Samson Njoroge ran a field hospital in a steep, rocky area of East Africa. He worked with carriers and wound dressers. The carriers had a dangerous job. They brought injured soldiers up and down the harsh slopes. Meanwhile, Njoroge trained the dressers and gave them tasks.

Field hospitals were often tent-like structures that ▶ temporarily housed soldiers before they were transferred to more permanent facilities.

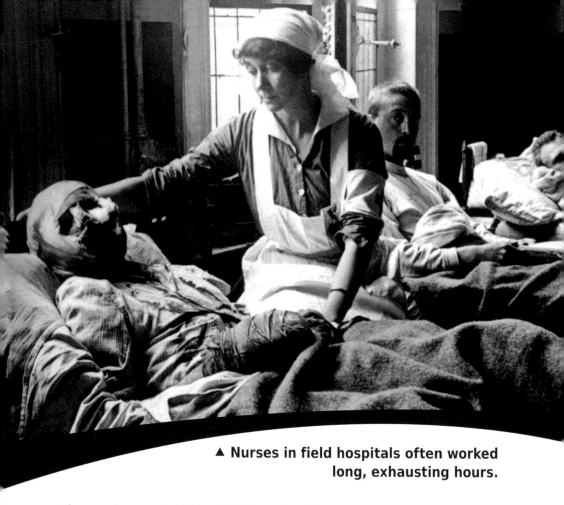

▲ **Nurses in field hospitals often worked long, exhausting hours.**

The carriers rushed in with injured soldiers. Njoroge watched as the dressers bathed and wrapped soldiers' wounds. He helped make sure the dressers worked quickly yet carefully.

Thousands of nurses also cared for soldiers. Maude Essig was one U.S. nurse stationed in France. She worked at a base hospital. This was a more permanent structure than a field hospital. Soldiers stayed there for a longer time. Yet, similar to Hayward, Essig worked long hours. On most days, she worked for more than 12 hours. Many times, she worked overnight.

Essig often had to deal with a lack of supplies. The hospital had no running water. Hospital workers carried buckets of water in from outside. Nurses emptied the buckets into bathtubs. They retrieved the water when they need to clean soldiers' wounds. They boiled the water first to remove bacteria.

After battles, Essig watched as workers carried wounded men on stretchers up eight flights of stairs. Then her work began. Essig cleaned dirt and grime from the men's wounds. She dressed the wounds with clean cloths. Often the wounded soldiers came in groups. Nurses struggled to keep up.

After a long day's work, Essig was exhausted. Yet she was happy to help the soldiers. "I feel I am really needed," she wrote.[6]

"These are busy nights and busier days . . . our patients are coming in directly from the front and they say it is terrible. . . . I see no one these days but my patients."

—Maude Essig, nurse[7]

Chapter 3

NEW DISCOVERIES

In the summer of 1914, Marie Curie was busy making preparations. A famous scientist, Curie was overseeing building plans. She planned to open her own laboratory in Paris, France. But when the war started in late July, Curie knew she had to change her plans.

In September 1914, Curie arrived in Paris after time away. Some areas of Paris were nearly empty.

◄ **Marie Curie drives a vehicle carrying a mobile X-ray unit.**

Young men had gone to fight in the war. Curie told her daughter, Irene, that they had a responsibility to help the soldiers however they could. "You and I, Irene, we will try to make ourselves useful," she wrote.[8]

Curie knew that X-rays could help doctors diagnose and treat soldiers' injuries. The physicist Wilhelm Roentgen had discovered X-rays in 1895. He found that X-rays could go through skin and muscle. They could not go through bone or lead. This characteristic allowed doctors to use X-rays to locate broken bones and **shrapnel**.

By the time of the war, X-ray machines were in hospitals around the world. Yet the hospitals were far from the battlefield. Curie knew of a way to bring X-ray machines to the soldiers. She transformed cars into traveling X-ray units. Irene and other volunteers helped her in this task.

The small cars contained screens, tubes, and cables used to produce the X-rays. Portable generators powered the X-ray units. Doctors, nurses, and medical students rode in the cars. They operated the equipment. Often Curie drove cars to the battlefield herself.

On her eighteenth birthday, Irene Curie spent the day on a battlefield. Guns and cannons fired in the distance. Irene operated X-ray equipment on wounded soldiers. She wrote to her mother about finding four parts of a shell in a soldier's hand. "I spent my birthday admirably," she wrote proudly.[9] Thanks to the X-ray equipment, surgeons could remove the shell fragments.

Field X-ray units were not the only new medical technology being used in the war. Another new technology involved **prosthetic limbs**. In 1917 surgeon David Silver ran a laboratory called the Limb Lab. Silver knew that many soldiers needed artificial limbs. They had lost arms or legs in battle. Yet many prosthetics at the time were made of wood. They were heavy and expensive. Silver was interested in producing cheaper, lighter limbs.

Working with factory owners, Silver and other scientists tested dozens of models and materials. Finally Silver found a model made of a lightweight material called vulcanized fiber. These prosthetic legs looked more like real legs. They were also more functional. Wearing the legs could help wounded men return to work after the war. The legs could even be worn with regular clothing from a store. Previous models had required special clothing. Silver began calling the model the Liberty Leg.

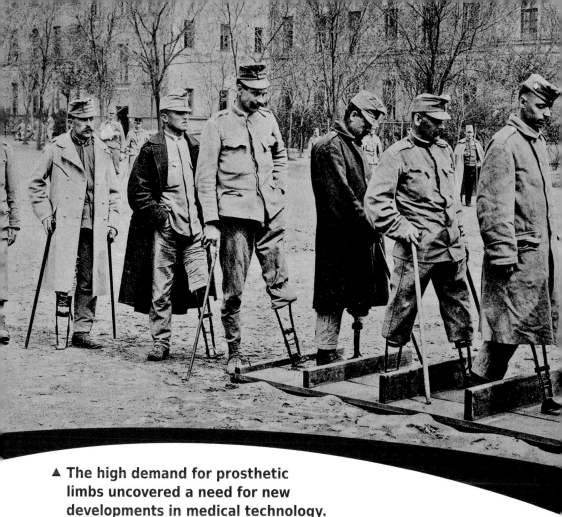

▲ The high demand for prosthetic limbs uncovered a need for new developments in medical technology.

Some soldiers complained about the Liberty Leg. Because it was created in a factory, it was available in only one size. As a result, some men found that the leg did not fit well. Yet the Liberty Leg was a first step toward prosthetic legs that were easier to use. In later decades, inventors improved on the Liberty Leg. They made lighter, more comfortable prosthetic legs.

Chapter 4

INFECTIONS AND DISEASES

In the winter of 1914 and 1915, Harry Roberts was a sergeant in the British Royal Army Medical Corps. Every day, Roberts had to walk through trenches filled with water. The weather was rainy and damp. Roberts walked in sopping wet boots. He watched as many men around him began to suffer from trench foot. This was a serious and painful condition.

◄ Soldiers who spent weeks in wet conditions could develop swollen limbs and experience nerve and tissue damage.

"Your feet swell up and go completely dead," said Roberts. "If . . . the swelling begins to go down, it is then that the agony begins. I have heard men cry and even scream with the pain."[10]

Doctors did not have many options for treating Roberts's fellow soldiers. They gave the soldiers aspirin to cope with the pain. For some men, it was too late. **Gangrene** had set in. Doctors amputated these soldiers' legs to help them survive.

Eventually the doctors realized they needed to take steps to prevent trench foot. Soldiers such as Roberts were ordered to wear rubber boots. These helped keep their feet dry. Officers gave the soldiers whale oil to rub on their legs and feet. Soldiers disliked the oil's fishy smell. But these steps were necessary to prevent trench foot.

Soldiers and civilians also faced threats from other diseases. In East Africa, many civilians worked as porters. They carried soldiers' equipment. Yet being near the battlefields exposed porters to serious diseases, such as malaria. Despite these dangers, porters had to keep working. "The work was dusty and heavy," said one porter. "No one spoke if he was ill or tired. It was all the same: work was work until nightfall. We paused only to sleep."[11]

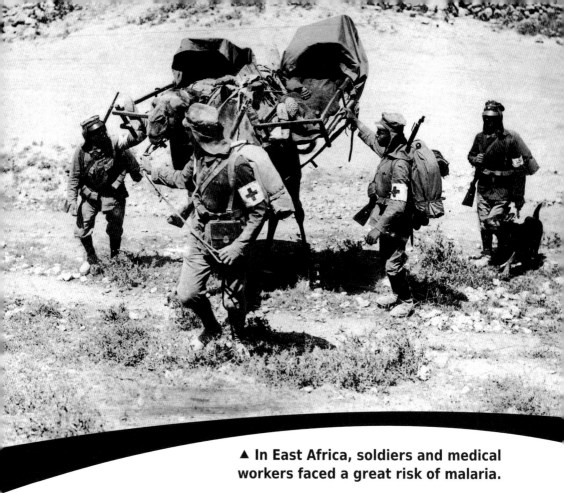

▲ **In East Africa, soldiers and medical workers faced a great risk of malaria.**

Diseases affected soldiers and medical workers from many countries. In January 1915, 25-year-old doctor Fred Davidson was traveling with a British military unit. Each day, the soldiers camped out in damp, dirty trenches. Bugs, mice, and rats infested the area. These creatures carried diseases and caused infection.

Davidson had been watching James Jack, an army captain. He thought the captain was ill. Jack had been shivering and looking pale. He layered on sweaters to keep himself warm.

Yet Jack refused to seek medical care. He wanted to keep fighting. Soon Davidson had to make a decision. He respected Jack's bravery. But he also believed a sick officer could spread disease to other men. Finally Davidson sent Jack a message.

▲ **During downtime, soldiers often hunted rats in trenches.**

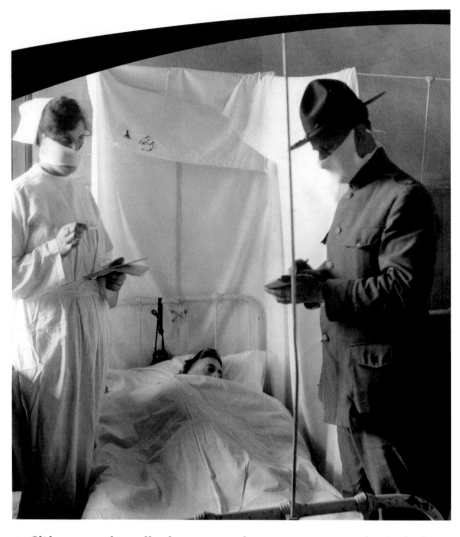

▲ **Citizens and medical personnel wore gauze masks to help stop the spread of the influenza epidemic.**

"What time will suit?" asked Davidson, trying to arrange an appointment. "No time would suit," Jack responded, refusing to meet.[12] Davidson had to speak with Philip Robertson, Jack's commanding officer. At last Robertson ordered Jack to leave.

The captain was sent to a hospital in Britain. There he was treated for severe influenza and pneumonia. But it was too late to keep the other men safe. Soon Robertson also had the influenza, or flu, virus.

Jack and Robertson were only two of many soldiers and officers who were dealing with diseases. As the war wound down in 1918, the influenza epidemic spread. "Medical science for four and one-half years devoted itself to putting men on the firing line," said scientists at the American Medical Association. "Now it must turn with its whole might to combating the greatest enemy of all—infectious disease."[13]

The flu was just one of many medical challenges that people continued to face after the war. Soldiers and civilians also continued to need care for other diseases, injuries, and infections.

"[Influenza] made everybody afraid to go see anybody. It changed a lot of society."

—William Sardo, an American infected by the flu virus during the flu epidemic[14]

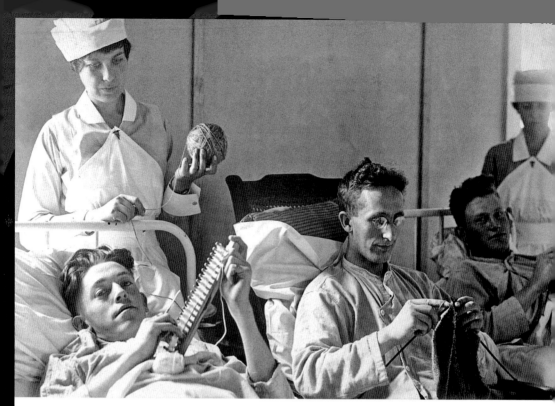

Chapter 5

AFTER THE WAR

On November 1, 1918, British Sergeant Major Arthur Cook was leading an army unit in a small village in France. Cook and his soldiers were dodging bullets from German forces. Suddenly a shell burst nearby, hitting Cook with shrapnel.

"I could scarcely believe I was wounded," Cook later recalled. "I had been dodging bullets for four years."[15] Ten days later, the war officially ended.

◄ The end of the war marked the beginning of a long recovery for many veterans.

Cook heard the news about the **armistice** from a hospital bed. His injury prevented him from celebrating. The fighting was over. But the hospitals were filled with wounded men. A total of 9 million soldiers had died in the war. An additional 21 million were injured. Many of these soldiers would need medical care for months or years. Hospitals, medical workers, and governments had to work together. They had to make sure the soldiers got the care they needed.

Maude Essig continued working at her base hospital in France. Soon after the armistice, 103 new patients were admitted. Some hospital staff had already left. Essig had little help treating the new patients. "All [patients] had to have beds, pajamas, bath robes, towels, blankets and all had to be fed," she wrote. "I had one nurse to help me . . . I did the ordering and dressed wounds as necessary."[16] Essig continued treating patients until March 1919. By that time, most of the soldiers had been released. Some were moved to other hospitals.

Marie Curie also continued her work after the war. After the armistice, she no longer needed to drive her field X-ray cars to battles. Instead, she taught courses to U.S. soldiers who were still in France. She showed the soldiers how to use X-ray machines.

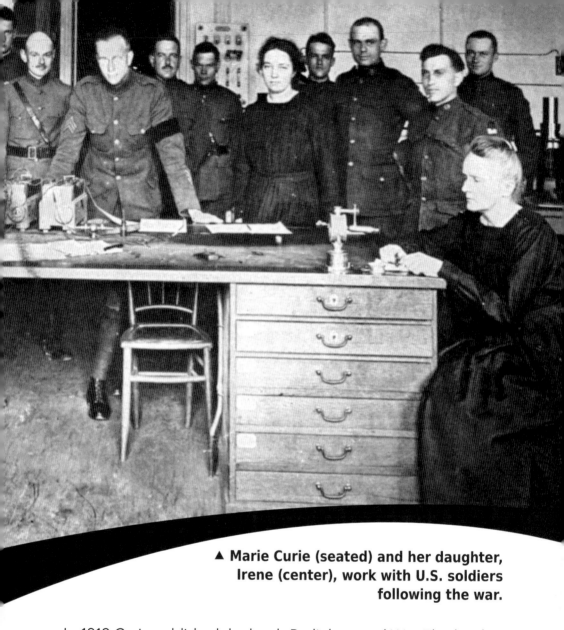

▲ **Marie Curie (seated) and her daughter, Irene (center), work with U.S. soldiers following the war.**

In 1919 Curie published the book *Radiology and War*. This book explained the importance of X-rays.

As Curie knew, World War I changed the field of medicine in many ways. For example, it pushed ahead research in many areas.

Scientists learned how to better treat diseases such as malaria and influenza. Researchers improved upon X-ray and prosthetic limb technologies. The war also helped countries be better prepared for dealing with large numbers of sick and injured people. First-aid treatment improved, and soldiers were more quickly transported to hospitals, allowing thousands more soldiers to survive.

World War I was deadly and tragic. Yet it also led to significant discoveries that would help many people in the future.

THINK ABOUT IT

- Chapter 1 describes new dangers on battlefields. How did medical inventions help workers respond to these dangers?
- Triage was first used in World War I. How did triage help improve medical care?
- Why were X-rays important for finding soldiers' injuries?
- What were some challenges that doctors, nurses, and soldiers faced after the war?

GLOSSARY

armistice (AHR-muh-stis): An armistice is a truce in which two sides agree to stop fighting for a time. On November 11, 1918, an armistice ended World War I.

epidemic (ep-i-DEM-ik): An epidemic is an illness that spreads quickly to many people. The flu epidemic of 1918 was very deadly.

front (FRUHNT): The front is the area where two military forces face off in combat. Doctors near the front faced many dangers.

gangrene (GANG-green): Gangrene is a type of infection. Doctors and soldiers had to use clean bandages to avoid gangrene.

prosthetic limbs (pros-THET-ik LIMZ): Prosthetic limbs are human-made devices that can substitute for missing arms and legs. Many injured soldiers required prosthetic limbs.

sanitation (san-i-TAY-shun): Sanitation is the use of clean practices. During the war, doctors used sanitation to prevent infection.

shells (SHELZ): Shells are explosive devices. Ambulance drivers often faced bursting shells around them.

shrapnel (SHRAP-nul): Shrapnel includes bullets or pieces of shells. Medical workers used X-rays to help find shrapnel in wounded soldiers.

trench warfare (TRENCH WAR-fare): During trench warfare, soldiers fight from long ditches. Trench warfare was common in World War I.

triage (TREE-azh): Triage is the practice of grouping soldiers based on how badly they need medical care. Using triage, doctors made sure soldiers with serious injuries were treated first.

SOURCE NOTES

1. "In the American Ambulance Field Service, 1916." *EyeWitness to History*. Ibis Communications, 2008. Web. 29 Apr. 2016.

2. Ibid.

3. James R. McConnell. "An American Ambulance in the Verdun Attack." *WWI Document Archive*. Brigham Young University, n.d. Web. 29 Apr. 2016.

4. "Battlefield Medics: Saving Lives under Fire." *HistoryNet*. World History Group, 12 Jun. 2006. Web. 30 Apr. 2016.

5. "WWI German Soldier Recalls Moment He Bayoneted Foe to Death." *The Telegraph*. Telegraph Media Group, 7 Mar. 2014. Web. 30 Apr. 2016.

6. Alma S. Woolley. "A Hoosier Nurse in France." *Indiana Magazine of History*. Indiana University, 2016. Web. 21 May 2016.

7. Ibid.

8. Susan Quinn. *Marie Curie: A Life*. New York: Simon & Schuster, 1995. Print. 356.

9. Barbara Goldsmith. *Obsessive Genius: The Inner World of Marie Curie*. New York: Norton, 2005. Print. 188.

10. Michael Freemantle. *The Chemists' War: 1914–1918*. Cambridge, UK: The Royal Society of Chemistry, 2014. Print. 127.

11. John Iliffe. *East African Doctors: A History of the Modern Profession*. Cambridge, UK: Cambridge UP, 1998. Print. 34–35.

12. Andrew Davidson. *A Doctor in the Great War*. New York: Marble Arch, 2014. Print. 232–233.

13. Molly Billings. "The Influenza Pandemic of 1918." *Human Virology at Stanford*. Robert Siegel, Feb. 2005. Web. 21 May 2016.

14. "Survivors Remember 1918 Global Flu Pandemic." *NBC News*. NBCNews.com, 2016. Web. 22 May 2016.

15. Richard van Emden. "A Very Bitter Victory: Returning WWI Soldiers' Hatred for the Leaders Who Let Them Die." *Daily Mail*. Associated Newspapers, 2008. Web. 14 May 2016.

16. Alma S. Woolley. "A Hoosier Nurse in France." *Indiana Magazine of History*. Indiana University, 2016. Web. 21 May 2016.

TO LEARN MORE

Books

Dowswell, Paul. *The Story of the First World War*. London, UK: Usborne, 2014.

Grant, R. G. *World War I: The Definitive Visual History*. New York: DK, 2014.

Kenney, Karen Latchana. *Everything World War I*. Washington, DC: National Geographic, 2014.

Web Sites

Visit our Web site for links about medicine in World War I: childsworld.com/links

Note to Parents, Teachers, and Librarians: We routinely verify our Web links to make sure they are safe and active sites. So encourage your readers to check them out!

INDEX